~A BINGO BOOK~

Ohio Bingo Book

COMPLETE BINGO GAME IN A BOOK

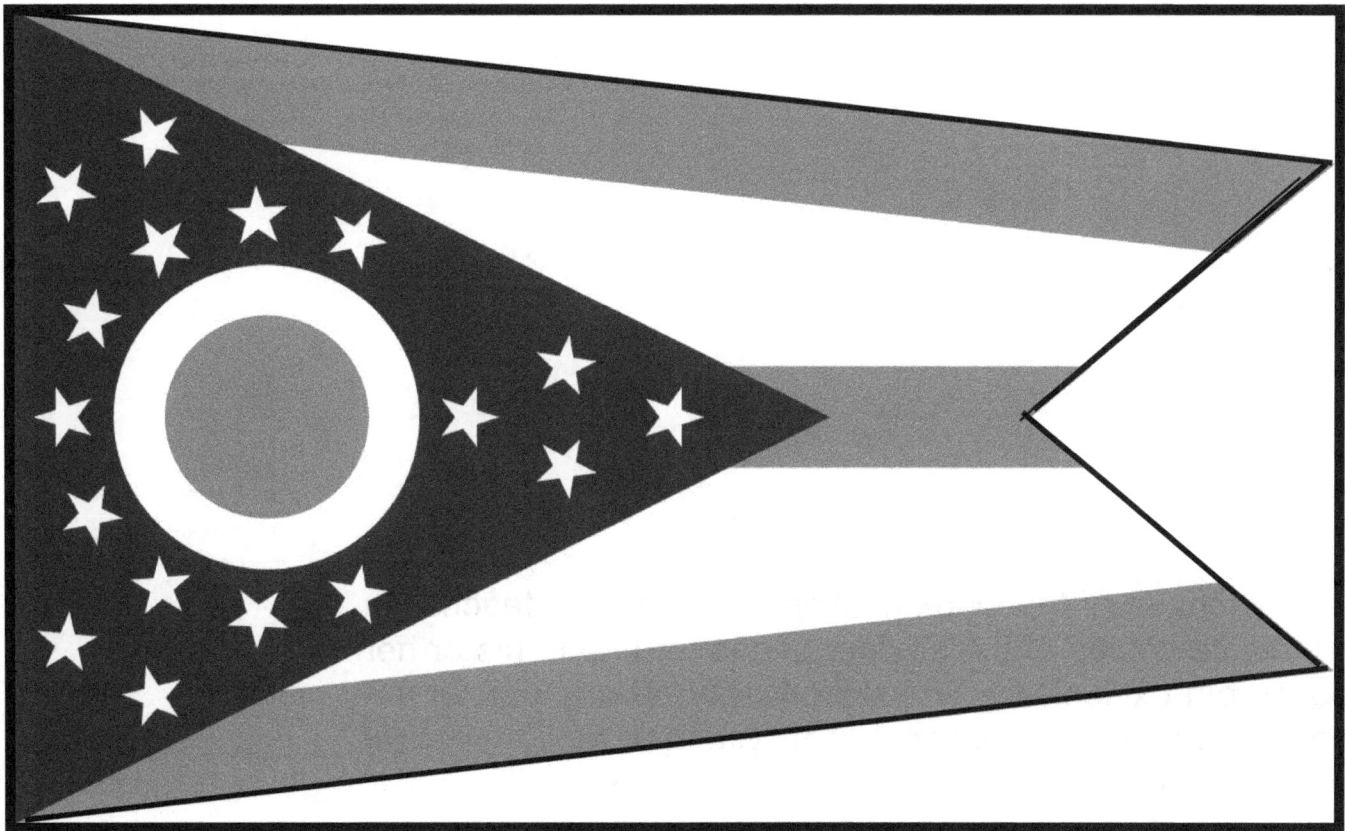

Written By Rebecca Stark

ISBN 978-0-87386-528-9

Educational Books 'n' Bingo

Printed in the U.S.A.

DIRECTIONS

INCLUDED:

List of Terms

Templates for Additional Terms and Clues

2 Clues per Term

30 Unique Bingo Cards

Markers

1. **Either cut apart the book or make copies of ALL the sheets. You might want to make an extra copy of the clue sheets to use for introduction and review. Keep the sheets in an envelope for easy reuse.**

2. Cut apart the call cards with terms and clues.

3. Pass out one bingo card per student. There are enough for a class of 30.

4. Pass out markers. You may cut apart the markers included in this book or use any other small items of your choice.

5. Decide whether or not you will require the entire card to be filled. Requiring the entire card to be filled provides a better review. However, if you have a short time to fill, you may prefer to have them do the just the border or some other format. Tell the class before you begin what is required.

6. There are 50 terms. Read the list before you begin. If there are any terms that have not been covered in class, you may want to read to the students the term and clues before you begin.

7. There is a blank space in the middle of each card. You can instruct the students to use it as a free space or you can write in answers to cover terms not included. Of course, in this case you would create your own clues. (Templates provided.)

8. Shuffle the cards and place them in a pile. Two or three clues are provided for each term. If you plan to play the game with the same group more than once, you might want to choose a different clue for each game. If not, you may choose to use more than one clue.

9. Be sure to keep the cards you have used for the present game in a separate pile. When a student calls, "Bingo," he or she will have to verify that the correct answers are on his or her card AND that the markers were placed in response to the proper questions. Pull out the cards that are on the student's card keeping them in the order they were used in the game. Read each clue as it was given and ask the student to identify the correct answer from his or her card.

10. If the student has the correct answers on the card AND has shown that they were marked in response to the *correct questions,* then that student is the winner and the game is over. If the student does not have the correct answers on the card OR he or she marked the answers in response to *the wrong questions,* then the game continues until there is a proper winner.

11. If you want to play again, reshuffle the cards and begin again.

Have fun!

TERMS INCLUDED

Agriculture (-al)

Akron

Appalachian Plateau

Astronaut(s)

Black Racer Snake

Bluegrass

Border(s)

Buckeye(s)

Canal(s)

Canton

Cincinnati

Cleveland

Columbus

County (-ies)

Crop(s)

Dayton

Robert de la Salle
    (René-Robert Cavelier, Sieur de La Salle)

Thomas Edison

Enabling Act of 1802

Executive Branch

Flag

French and Indian War

Great Lakes Plains

Highest Point

Industry

Iroquois

Thomas Jefferson

Judicial Branch

Lake Erie Shoreline

Manufacturing

Legislative Branch

Mother of Presidents

Motto(-es)

New France

Northwest Ordinance

Northwest Territory

Ohio Oil Rush

Pontiac

Railroad(s)

River(s)

Sandusky

Seal

Sheriden Cave

Till Plains

Toledo

Treaty of Greeneville

Treaty of Paris

Underground Railroad

Union

Orville Wright

Ohio Bingo

Additional Terms

Choose as many additional terms as you would like and write them in the squares. Repeat each as desired.
Cut out the squares and randomly distribute them to the class.
Instruct the students to place their square on the center space of their card.

Ohio Bingo

Clues for Additional Terms

Write two or three clues for each of your additional terms.

_____ 1. 2. 3.	_____ 1. 2. 3.
_____ 1. 2. 3.	_____ 1. 2. 3.
_____ 1. 2. 3.	_____ 1. 2. 3.

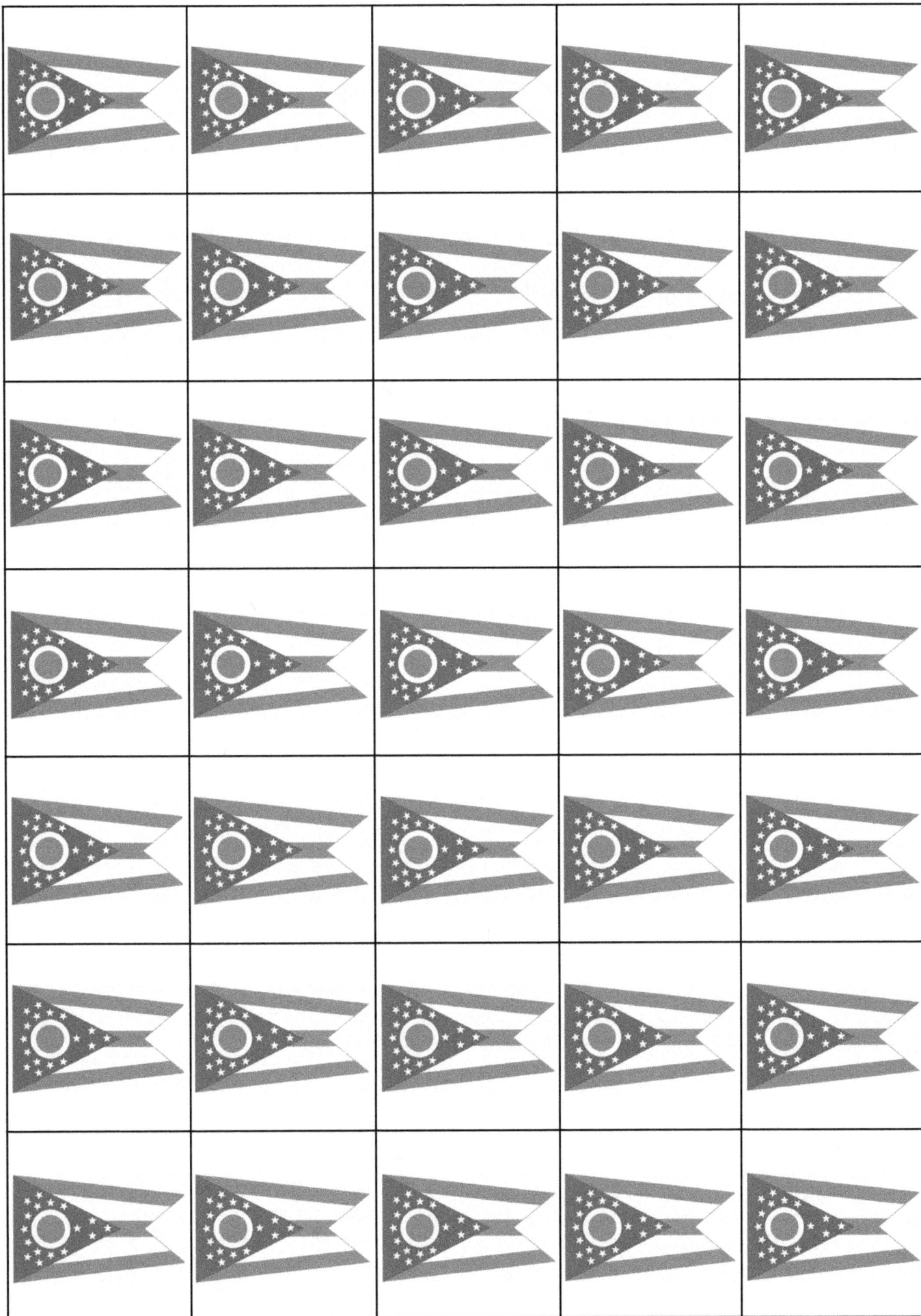

Agriculture (-al) 1. The ___ and food processing industries are important in the state. Soybeans and corn for grain are the leading cash crops. 2. Most early industries in the state had ___ roots. For example, Cincinnati became an important pork processing center.	**Akron** 1. During most of the1900s ___ was considered the Rubber Capital of the World. 2. Four major tire companies were headquartered in ___ in the 1900s: Goodrich Corporation, Goodyear Tire and Rubber Company, Firestone Tire and Rubber Company, and General Tire.
Appalachian Plateau 1. The ___ covers the eastern half of Ohio, south of the Lake Erie Plains. 2. The northern part of the ___ consists of rolling hills and valleys. The southern two-thirds consists of steep hills and valleys. The ___ is the most rugged area in the state.	**Astronaut(s)** 1. These ___ were born in Ohio: John Glenn, Neil Armstrong, Jim Lovell, and Judith Resnick. 2. ___ Neil Armstrong, the first person to walk on the moon, was born in Wapakoneta, Ohio, on August 5, 1930.
Black Racer Snake 1. The ___ is the state reptile. 2. This common reptile has smooth scales; its chin, throat and jaw are white or gray .	**Bluegrass** 1. The ___ Region continues north from Kentucky and consists of hilly and gently rolling land. Cincinnati is in this region of Ohio. 2. The ___ Region comprises a small, triangular area of land in southern Ohio. The soil is thin and not very fertile.
Border(s) 1. These states ___ Ohio: Pennsylvania, West Virginia, Kentucky, Indiana, and Michigan. 2. Lake Erie ___ Ohio to the north.	**Buckeye(s)** 1. Ohio is called the ___ State. Ohioans are sometimes called ___. 2. Ohio's state tree is the ___.
Canal(s) 1. A 1000-mile network of navigable ___ was constructed in Ohio between 1825 and 1847. They provided a system of economical transportation. 2. The Ohio and Erie ___ ran from Cleveland to Portsmouth. The Miami & Erie ___ ran from Toledo to Cincinnati.	**Canton** 1. The Football Hall of Fame is located in ___. 2. President McKinley lived In ___. He practiced as an attorney there and conducted his political campaigns from there. The McKinley National Memorial is located in ___.

Ohio Bingo

© Barbara M. Peller

Cincinnati 1. ___ was settled in 1788; it is located on the north bank of the Ohio River at the Ohio-Kentucky border. 2. Over-the-Rhine is a neighborhood in ___. It contains the largest collection of 19th-century Italianate architecture still standing in the United States.	**Cleveland** 1. ___ is the county seat of Cuyahoga County, the most populous county in the state. 2. ___ is the second largest city in Ohio after Columbus. Greater ___ is the largest metropolitan area.
Columbus 1. ___ is the capital and largest city of Ohio. 2. Ohio State University is a public research university. Its main campus is in ___.	**County (-ies)** 1. There are 88 ___ in Ohio. 2. Except for Summit and Cuyahoga, ___ in Ohio have a 3-person board of commissioners as well as several other elected officials. Summit and Cuyahoga have a ___ executive and a ___ council.
Crop(s) 1. Important ___ include corn, soybeans, winter wheat, hay, tomatoes for processing, apples, grapes, poinsettias, mushrooms, and maple syrup. 2. Corn and soybeans are the top ___.	**Dayton** 1. Wright-Patterson Air Force Base is near the city of ___. 2. The Vectren ___ Air Show takes place annually at the ___ International Airport. It is one of the largest air shows in the nation.
Robert de la Salle (René-Robert Cavelier, Sieur de La Salle) 1. On April 9, 1682, ___ claimed all of the Mississippi River Basin for France and named it Louisiana in honor of the French king. 2. ___ was the first European to sail down the Mississippi River to the Gulf of Mexico.	**Thomas Edison** 1. This famous inventor was born in Milan, Ohio, in 1847. 2. ___'s inventions included the phonograph, the motion-picture camera, and a practical electric light bulb.
Enabling Act of 1802 1. The ___ authorized the residents of the eastern portion of the Northwest Territory to form the state of Ohio. 2. This act called for the admittance of Ohio as a state as soon as possible.	**Executive Branch** 1. The governor is the head of the ___. The governor and lieutenant governor are elected on one ticket. 2. Like the governor and lieutenant governor, the governor's cabinet, the secretary of state, the attorney general, the auditor, and the treasurer are part of the ___.

Ohio Bingo

Flag

1. Ohio's red, white and blue ___ has a unique swallowtail pennant design. It was designed by John Eisemann.
2. The blue triangle on the ___ has 13 stars around a circle; they represent the original 13 states. There are also 4 stars near the center because Ohio was the 17th state.

French and Indian War

1. During the ___, the Iroquois Confederacy sided with the British against the French and their Algonquian allies.
2. Competition over control of the Ohio Country was a primary cause of the ___. Both the English and the French claimed the land west of the Appalachian Mountains.

Great Lakes Plains

1. The ___ geographic region is in the north, where Ohio borders Lake Erie.
2. The fertile lowland of the ___ runs along the Great Lakes from Wisconsin to Ohio. In northeast Ohio this region is referred to as the Lake Erie Plains.

Highest Point

1. At 1,549 feet, Campbell Hill is the ___ in the state.
2. Campbell Hill, the ___ in Ohio, is in the city of Bellefontaine. It is is the former site of the Bellefontaine Air Force Station.

Industry

1. The solar energy ___ is important, especially in Toledo. The aerospace ___ is important, especially in Dayton.
2. Bioscience, including health care, is an important ___. Manufacturing, mining of oil and natural gas, and agriculture are also important.

Iroquois

1. By 1650, the ___ had moved into Ohio Country. They drove out other groups of Native Americans living in the area.
2. The Beaver Wars occurred because the ___ wanted to expand their territory and monopolize the fur trade.

Thomas Jefferson

1. ___ was President when Ohio became the seventeenth state in 1803.
2. ___ was President when the Louisiana Purchase took place.

Judicial Branch

1. The ___ interprets what our laws mean and makes decisions about the laws and those who break them.
2. It is made up of the Courts of Common Pleas; the District Courts of Appeals; and the Supreme Court of Ohio, which is the highest.

Lake Erie Shoreline

1. The ___ runs from Conneaut in the east to Toledo in the west.
2. The eastern part of the ___ consists of ten- to eighteen-foot clay bluffs. The western part consists of beaches of clay and sand.

Legislative Branch

1. The General Assembly is the ___ of government; it comprises the Senate and the House of Representatives.
2. The ___ makes the laws.

Ohio Bingo

Manufacturing 1. Much of Ohio's ___ activity is within the transportation segment, including the assembly of automobiles and trucks and parts for these motor vehicles and for aircraft. 2. ___ of steel, chemicals, and plastics is also important.	**Mother of Presidents** 1. Ohio is sometimes called the ___ because Ulysses S. Grant, Rutherford B. Hayes, James Garfield, Benjamin Harrison, William McKinley, William Howard Taft, and Warren Harding were all born here. 2. Ohio is sometimes called the ___ because 7 Presidents were born here.
Motto(-es) 1. The state ___ is "With God, all things are possible." 2. State ___ reflect the character and beliefs of the citizens of the state at the time they were adopted.	**New France** 1. Ohio Country became part of ___ in 1663. 2. Canada was the most developed colony of ___.
Northwest Ordinance 1. The ___ created the first organized territory in the United States, with a civil government under the jurisdiction of the Congress. 2. Ohio was the first state admitted to the Union under the ___, which was passed on July 13, 1787.	**Northwest Territory** 1. The Northwest Ordinance created the ___, which comprised the present-day states of Ohio, Michigan, Indiana, Illinois, and Wisconsin. 2. The ___ existed from July 13, 1787, until March 1, 1803, when the southeastern portion of the territory was admitted to the Union as the state of Ohio.
Ohio Oil Rush 1. The ___ was a 19th-century petroleum boom in Ohio. 2. This refers to the years between 1895 and 1903 when Ohio was the leading producer of crude oil in the country.	**Pontiac** 1. ___ was an Ottawa Indian chief who organized a combined resistance to British power in the Great Lakes area. 2. Chief ___ of the Ottawa Indians encouraged Ohio Country natives to rise up. They attacked Fort Detroit in May 1763, marking the beginning of the conflict known as ___'s Rebellion.
Railroad(s) 1. ___ construction was underway in Ohio by the mid-19th century, and by 1860 Ohio had more miles of track than any other state. 2. The Little Miami ___ was one of Ohio's most important early ___. It connected Cincinnati to Springfield. Ohio Bingo	**River(s)** 1. The Ohio, Cuyahoga, Miami, and Sandusky are major ___ in Ohio. 2. By volume the Ohio ___ is the largest tributary of the Mississippi ___. © Barbara M. Peller

Sandusky 1. Fort ___ was a small British fort in the Ohio Country; it was built on the shore of Lake Erie in present-day Ohio. 2. Fort ___ was built and used by British troops in the Ohio Country during Pontiac's Rebellion and the French and Indian War.	**Seal** 1. The Scioto River is depicted on the Great ___ of Ohio. 2. The sheaf of wheat on the Great ___, represents agriculture. The 17 arrows symbolize Ohio as the 17th state to join the Union.
Sheriden Cave 1. Evidence of life in the late Ice Age is preserved at the ___ site in Wyandot County. 2. Bones of many different extinct animal species were found at ___.	**Till Plains** 1. The ___ start in Ohio south of Lake Erie Plains and expand westward. They are characterized by gently rolling hills. 2. The ___ landscape is one of the most fertile farming regions in the nation. The Corn Belt begins in the ___.
Toledo 1. ___ is the fourth most populous city in Ohio after Columbus, Cincinnati, and Cleveland. 2. The Miami and Erie Canal connected the Ohio River in Cincinnati with Lake Erie in ___.	**Treaty of Greeneville** 1. This treaty set a boundary between Indian lands and lands open to white settlement. 2. As a result of the ___, the Miami Indians, the Wyandot Indians, the Shawnee Indians, the Delaware Indians, and other tribes gave up their rights to lands in the southeastern portion of the Northwest Territory.
Treaty of Paris 1. The ___ of 1763 ended the French and Indian War. 2. With the signing of the ___, France ceded its possessions in modern-day Canada and most of the territory east of the Mississippi River.	**Underground Railroad** 1. The ___ was a system of safe houses and hiding places connecting the slaveholding South to freedom in Canada. 2. Although a free state, Ohio was a dangerous stop along the ___.
Union 1. Before Ohio was admitted to the ___ on March 1, 1803, it was part of the Northwest Territory. 2. When Ohio was admitted to the ___, it became the 17th state.	**Orville Wright** 1. This pioneer in aviation was born in Dayton. 2. He and his brother Wilbur invented and built the world's first successful airplane.

Ohio Bingo

Ohio Bingo

River(s)	Akron	Astronaut(s)	Executive Branch	Bluegrass
Thomas Edison	Appalachian Plateau	Orville Wright	Mother of Presidents	Sheriden Cave
Union	Legislative Branch		Ohio Oil Rush	Manufacturing
Underground Railroad	Seal	Treaty of Paris	Agriculture (-al)	New France
Northwest Territory	Great Lakes Plains	Crop(s)	Toledo	Iroquois

Ohio Bingo: Card No. 1

Ohio Bingo

Underground Railroad	Union	Industry	Sandusky	Judicial Branch
New France	Dayton	Canal(s)	Seal	Northwest Ordinance
Cincinnati	Great Lakes Plains		Highest Point	Treaty of Paris
Pontiac	Railroad(s)	Legislative Branch	Agriculture (-al)	Bluegrass
Sheriden Cave	Orville Wright	Crop(s)	Thomas Edison	Toledo

Ohio Bingo: Card No. 2

Ohio Bingo

Great Lakes Plains	Treaty of Paris	Dayton	Agriculture (-al)	Union
New France	Appalachian Plateau	Canton	Akron	French and Indian War
Seal	Orville Wright		Northwest Ordinance	Black Racer Snake
Legislative Branch	Cincinnati	Northwest Territory	Pontiac	Industry
Toledo	Cleveland	Crop(s)	Judicial Branch	Lake Erie Shoreline

Ohio Bingo

Legislative Branch	Northwest Ordinance	Astronaut(s)	Cleveland	Lake Erie Shoreline
Motto(-es)	Buckeye(s)	Akron	Sandusky	Union
Ohio Oil Rush	Pontiac		Iroquois	Executive Branch
Treaty of Paris	Northwest Territory	Orville Wright	Crop(s)	Canal(s)
Columbus	Sheriden Cave	Border(s)	Toledo	Manufacturing

Ohio Bingo: Card No. 4

Ohio Bingo

Sheriden Cave	Bluegrass	Seal	Canal(s)	Cleveland
Motto(-es)	Treaty of Paris	Canton	Highest Point	Appalachian Plateau
Astronaut(s)	Manufacturing		Mother of Presidents	Flag
Iroquois	Judicial Branch	River(s)	Lake Erie Shoreline	County (-ies)
Dayton	Crop(s)	Union	Legislative Branch	Ohio Oil Rush

Ohio Bingo

Black Racer Snake	Northwest Ordinance	Industry	Lake Erie Shoreline	Manufacturing
Judicial Branch	Seal	County (-ies)	Akron	Union
Sandusky	Columbus		Buckeye(s)	Highest Point
Crop(s)	Northwest Territory	Agriculture (-al)	Border(s)	Astronaut(s)
New France	Canal(s)	River(s)	Ohio Oil Rush	Robert de la Salle

Ohio Bingo

River(s)	Northwest Ordinance	Flag	Treaty of Paris	Dayton
New France	Lake Erie Shoreline	Great Lakes Plains	Appalachian Plateau	Motto(-es)
Manufacturing	Executive Branch		Highest Point	Buckeye(s)
Legislative Branch	Pontiac	Canton	Underground Railroad	Cincinnati
Crop(s)	Cleveland	Agriculture (-al)	Border(s)	Black Racer Snake

Ohio Bingo: Card No. 7

Ohio Bingo

Ohio Oil Rush	Northwest Ordinance	Enabling Act of 1802	Agriculture (-al)	Buckeye(s)
Motto(-es)	Astronaut(s)	Sandusky	Manufacturing	Canal(s)
Robert de la Salle	Cleveland		Lake Erie Shoreline	Bluegrass
Toledo	Legislative Branch	Underground Railroad	Columbus	Pontiac
Orville Wright	Crop(s)	Border(s)	Seal	New France

Ohio Bingo: Card No. 8

Ohio Bingo

Highest Point	Dayton	Great Lakes Plains	Robert de la Salle	Cleveland
Columbus	Agriculture (-al)	Ohio Oil Rush	Seal	Northwest Ordinance
French and Indian War	River(s)		Appalachian Plateau	Enabling Act of 1802
County (-ies)	Bluegrass	Northwest Territory	Mother of Presidents	Flag
Pontiac	Lake Erie Shoreline	Canton	Underground Railroad	Iroquois

Ohio Bingo: Card No. 9

Ohio Bingo

Underground Railroad	Thomas Jefferson	Buckeye(s)	Sandusky	Robert de la Salle
Manufacturing	Canal(s)	Akron	Appalachian Plateau	Lake Erie Shoreline
Cleveland	Northwest Ordinance		Executive Branch	Cincinnati
Northwest Territory	Iroquois	County (-ies)	Judicial Branch	French and Indian War
Canton	New France	Industry	Sheriden Cave	Ohio Oil Rush

Ohio Bingo

Black Racer Snake	Northwest Ordinance	Seal	County (-ies)	New France
Enabling Act of 1802	French and Indian War	Mother of Presidents	Highest Point	Akron
Motto(-es)	Judicial Branch		Industry	Great Lakes Plains
Canton	Union	Lake Erie Shoreline	Cleveland	Underground Railroad
Columbus	Crop(s)	River(s)	Border(s)	Dayton

Ohio Bingo

Dayton	Bluegrass	French and Indian War	Lake Erie Shoreline	Highest Point
Great Lakes Plains	New France	Astronaut(s)	Border(s)	Appalachian Plateau
River(s)	Flag		Manufacturing	Sandusky
Crop(s)	Pontiac	Judicial Branch	Underground Railroad	Motto(-es)
Northwest Ordinance	Enabling Act of 1802	Cleveland	Columbus	Canal(s)

Ohio Bingo

County (-ies)	Bluegrass	Black Racer Snake	French and Indian War	Manufacturing
Astronaut(s)	Enabling Act of 1802	Thomas Jefferson	Highest Point	Cincinnati
Agriculture (-al)	Canal(s)		Great Lakes Plains	Flag
Ohio Oil Rush	Judicial Branch	Buckeye(s)	Cleveland	Underground Railroad
Crop(s)	Iroquois	Border(s)	River(s)	Mother of Presidents

Ohio Bingo: Card No. 13

© Barbara M. Peller

Ohio Bingo

Thomas Edison	Judicial Branch	Seal	Highest Point	Columbus
Canal(s)	River(s)	French and Indian War	Appalachian Plateau	Northwest Ordinance
County (-ies)	Executive Branch		Industry	Canton
Iroquois	Agriculture (-al)	Cleveland	Buckeye(s)	Black Racer Snake
Crop(s)	Sandusky	Cincinnati	New France	Ohio Oil Rush

Ohio Bingo: Card No. 14

Ohio Bingo

Mother of Presidents	Highest Point	Seal	Dayton	Thomas Jefferson
Black Racer Snake	Industry	Akron	Astronaut(s)	Columbus
Manufacturing	River(s)		Union	Northwest Ordinance
Crop(s)	French and Indian War	Enabling Act of 1802	Lake Erie Shoreline	County (-ies)
New France	Pontiac	Border(s)	Robert de la Salle	Great Lakes Plains

Ohio Bingo: Card No. 15

Ohio Bingo

Buckeye(s)	French and Indian War	Enabling Act of 1802	Robert de la Salle	Railroad(s)
Sandusky	Cincinnati	Flag	Motto(-es)	Executive Branch
County (-ies)	Bluegrass		Manufacturing	Great Lakes Plains
Legislative Branch	Canal(s)	Crop(s)	Mother of Presidents	Underground Railroad
Columbus	Treaty of Greeneville	Border(s)	Pontiac	Northwest Ordinance

Ohio Bingo

Canton	Till Plains	Thomas Jefferson	French and Indian War	Thomas Edison
Mother of Presidents	Columbus	Agriculture (-al)	Executive Branch	Flag
Highest Point	Ohio Oil Rush		Treaty of Greeneville	Enabling Act of 1802
Iroquois	New France	Underground Railroad	Seal	Cincinnati
Northwest Territory	County (-ies)	Dayton	Judicial Branch	Bluegrass

Ohio Bingo

Robert de la Salle	Cleveland	Canal(s)	County (-ies)	Sandusky
Northwest Ordinance	Canton	Northwest Territory	Manufacturing	Columbus
Highest Point	Cincinnati		Thomas Jefferson	Astronaut(s)
Bluegrass	Akron	Judicial Branch	Underground Railroad	Industry
Treaty of Greeneville	French and Indian War	Seal	Till Plains	Black Racer Snake

Ohio Bingo: Card No. 18

Ohio Bingo

Manufacturing	Black Racer Snake	French and Indian War	Enabling Act of 1802	Underground Railroad
Mother of Presidents	Thomas Jefferson	Northwest Ordinance	Dayton	Executive Branch
Till Plains	Cleveland		Appalachian Plateau	Union
Industry	Treaty of Greeneville	Northwest Territory	Pontiac	Lake Erie Shoreline
Astronaut(s)	Railroad(s)	New France	Ohio Oil Rush	Border(s)

Ohio Bingo

Thomas Edison	Till Plains	Thomas Jefferson	French and Indian War	Border(s)
Canal(s)	Great Lakes Plains	Motto(-es)	Northwest Territory	Sandusky
Bluegrass	Flag		Legislative Branch	Akron
Sheriden Cave	Orville Wright	Toledo	Pontiac	Treaty of Greeneville
Treaty of Paris	Ohio Oil Rush	Railroad(s)	Underground Railroad	Agriculture (-al)

Ohio Bingo

Mother of Presidents	Black Racer Snake	Motto(-es)	French and Indian War	Sheriden Cave
Bluegrass	Thomas Jefferson	Buckeye(s)	Enabling Act of 1802	River(s)
Cincinnati	New France		Till Plains	Seal
Northwest Territory	Dayton	Treaty of Greeneville	Iroquois	Ohio Oil Rush
Legislative Branch	Railroad(s)	Border(s)	Canton	Pontiac

Ohio Bingo

Robert de la Salle	Industry	Thomas Jefferson	Astronaut(s)	County (-ies)
Sandusky	Judicial Branch	Union	Enabling Act of 1802	Appalachian Plateau
Canal(s)	Executive Branch		River(s)	Flag
Treaty of Greeneville	Iroquois	Pontiac	Akron	Motto(-es)
Railroad(s)	Canton	Till Plains	Cincinnati	Orville Wright

Ohio Bingo

Buckeye(s)	Till Plains	Dayton	Astronaut(s)	Border(s)
Black Racer Snake	Thomas Edison	New France	Mother of Presidents	Akron
Industry	County (-ies)		Toledo	River(s)
Cincinnati	Railroad(s)	Treaty of Greeneville	Canton	Pontiac
Sheriden Cave	Orville Wright	Ohio Oil Rush	Northwest Territory	Thomas Jefferson

Ohio Bingo: Card No. 23

Ohio Bingo

Buckeye(s)	Ohio Oil Rush	Thomas Edison	Till Plains	Enabling Act of 1802
Thomas Jefferson	Border(s)	Motto(-es)	Sandusky	River(s)
Flag	Robert de la Salle		County (-ies)	Cincinnati
Sheriden Cave	Toledo	Treaty of Greeneville	Canton	Bluegrass
Treaty of Paris	Legislative Branch	Railroad(s)	Agriculture (-al)	Orville Wright

Ohio Bingo

Legislative Branch	Motto(-es)	Till Plains	Seal	Thomas Jefferson
Akron	Bluegrass	Mother of Presidents	Buckeye(s)	Appalachian Plateau
Iroquois	Enabling Act of 1802		Toledo	Treaty of Greeneville
Union	Sheriden Cave	Orville Wright	Railroad(s)	Executive Branch
Border(s)	Thomas Edison	Canal(s)	Columbus	Treaty of Paris

Ohio Bingo

Thomas Jefferson	Till Plains	Industry	Sandusky	Robert de la Salle
Northwest Territory	Judicial Branch	Enabling Act of 1802	Thomas Edison	Buckeye(s)
Iroquois	Toledo		Executive Branch	Legislative Branch
Canton	Astronaut(s)	Sheriden Cave	Railroad(s)	Treaty of Greeneville
Flag	Columbus	Seal	Orville Wright	Treaty of Paris

Ohio Bingo

Industry	Canal(s)	Till Plains	Thomas Edison	Great Lakes Plains
Sheriden Cave	Toledo	Mother of Presidents	Treaty of Greeneville	Appalachian Plateau
Judicial Branch	Orville Wright		Railroad(s)	Legislative Branch
Robert de la Salle	Black Racer Snake	Motto(-es)	Treaty of Paris	Akron
Columbus	Executive Branch	Thomas Jefferson	Union	Flag

Ohio Bingo: Card No. 27

Ohio Bingo

Industry	Thomas Edison	Union	Till Plains	Buckeye(s)
Great Lakes Plains	Thomas Jefferson	Toledo	Sandusky	Executive Branch
Orville Wright	Cincinnati		Flag	Northwest Territory
Underground Railroad	Robert de la Salle	New France	Railroad(s)	Treaty of Greeneville
Astronaut(s)	Highest Point	Columbus	Treaty of Paris	Sheriden Cave

Ohio Bingo

Agriculture (-al)	Thomas Edison	Robert de la Salle	Mother of Presidents	Highest Point
Pontiac	Northwest Territory	Motto(-es)	Flag	Union
Iroquois	Toledo		Appalachian Plateau	Till Plains
Great Lakes Plains	Sheriden Cave	Lake Erie Shoreline	Railroad(s)	Treaty of Greeneville
Buckeye(s)	Enabling Act of 1802	Treaty of Paris	Black Racer Snake	Orville Wright

Ohio Bingo: Card No. 29

Ohio Bingo

Cleveland	Till Plains	Sandusky	Highest Point	Treaty of Greeneville
Akron	Thomas Edison	Industry	Executive Branch	Appalachian Plateau
Iroquois	County (-ies)		Flag	Motto(-es)
Treaty of Paris	Black Racer Snake	Astronaut(s)	Railroad(s)	Toledo
Sheriden Cave	Manufacturing	Orville Wright	Agriculture (-al)	Union